SOUTHDOWN BUSES

Best Wishes
Mick Hymans

SOUTHDOWN BUSES

MICHAEL HYMANS

AMBERLEY

First published 2016

Amberley Publishing
The Hill, Stroud
Gloucestershire, GL5 4EP

www.amberley-books.com

Copyright © Michael Hymans, 2016

The right of Michael Hymans to be identified as the Author of this work has been asserted in accordance with the Copyrights, Designs and Patents Act 1988.

ISBN 978 1 4456 6300 5 (print)
ISBN 978 1 4456 6301 2 (ebook)

All rights reserved. No part of this book may be reprinted or reproduced or utilised in any form or by any electronic, mechanical or other means, now known or hereafter invented, including photocopying and recording, or in any information storage or retrieval system, without the permission in writing from the Publishers.

British Library Cataloguing in Publication Data.
A catalogue record for this book is available from the British Library.

Typesetting by Amberley Publishing.
Printed in the UK.

Contents

Preface   4

A Brief History   5

The Singles   9

The Doubles   60

Open-Toppers   120

Preface

This book came about because I acquired an amazing collection of photographs of Southdown vehicles taken in the 1950s. There were over 400 images, all taken by one man – Peter Funnell, of Seaford. Together with his friend, Peter would cycle to various locations to photograph his beloved Southdown buses. No Eastbourne Corporation or Brighton buses for him though; only Southdowns were recorded.

In the mid-1950s, Peter tried to join the navy; his eyesight let him down, but he did join the NAAFI canteens and went to sea. This curtailed his photographic exploits but, when arriving back in dock at Portsmouth, he took the opportunity to record Southdowns in that area.

The photographs are not only a superb record of the Southdown fleet, but also capture evocative shots of shops, street furniture, fashions and passing traffic – much of which are no longer with us. Peter never had any of his work published, and so all the photographs included here can be enjoyed by the public for the very first time. Peter did, however, buy some photographs for his collection, including some images captured by Mr A. M. Lambert, who has kindly given me permission to use them. I must also thank Mr Lambert for the superb booklets he has produced for the Southdown Enthusiasts Club, from where many of the facts in the captions have been gleaned.

I do not think I have infringed anybody's copyright, but if I have, I apologise. If my apologies are not enough, please contact me.

Much has been written about the history of Southdown and I cannot add anything to that, except to re-iterate that they were a byword for comfort and service. The images included here will speak louder than words.

A Brief History

Southdown Motor Services was formed in 1915 by the amalgamation of three other companies – the London & South Coast Haulage Services, Worthing Motor Services and the country routes of the Brighton, Hove & Preston United Omnibus Company. Their original headquarters was at Middle Street, Brighton, but this changed to 5 Steine Street, Brighton – also the location of the coach station.

Although their first services were in the Brighton area, they soon expanded by introducing their own new routes and purchasing other operators, taking over their services. One of these was Chapman's of Eastbourne, who had been running horse-drawn buses since the nineteenth century. Eastbourne Borough Council started their local motor-bus services in 1903 so Chapman concentrated on excursions and tours using his fleet of charabancs, being the first operator in the country to offer inclusive breaks of transport with hotels paid for when he ran a trip to Cornwall in 1911. Further tours ensued, with Scotland being visited before he ventured to the Continent with trips as far as Italy in the early 1920s. Southdown utilised his knowledge and reputation to extend their coaching activities, also expanding westward through the acquisition of Horndean and the Southsea Tourist Company Ltd.

The company started running express coach services, with its first destination being London in 1921. In those days the destination was Lupus Street, but when Victoria coach station opened in 1932 it was a Southdown coach that was the first vehicle to enter. The network of express services expanded with services from London serving Hastings, Eastbourne, Newhaven and Seaford, Worthing, Bognor, Littlehampton, Portsmouth and Southampton on the south coast. Not all express services started and finished in the capital, however. A service also ran to Cheltenham, where connections could be made with services to Wales and the Midlands. Over 150 bus services operated, ranging from short journeys within a particular town to longer ones connecting towns several miles apart, which also served many of the villages in between that would otherwise have had no public transport.

Although they took over many smaller operators, they worked with larger adjacent bus companies. They entered into a joint venture with Maidstone & District in 1921 to operate through bus services between each other's areas. The joint service between

Brighton and Gravesend was the longest bus route in the country and it necessitated crews from the respective companies driving each other's vehicles, as a full return journey could not be completed in a day's work.

Shorter routes crossing into M&D's territory were run alternately. These included the 180 route from Brighton to Hastings via Lewes and Heathfield, route 191 from Eastbourne to Tunbridge Wells and route 99 from Eastbourne to Hastings. Other agreements were made with Hants & Dorset with services to Southampton and Winchester.

In 1929, they joined forces with both the East Kent Road Car Company and Hants & Dorset to run a coastal coach service from Margate all the way to Bournemouth. This was marketed under the name of the South Coast Express and continued into NBC ownership. Not all relationships with rivals were that friendly though. There was a long, drawn-out battle with Eastbourne Corporation over the right to operate to the top of Beachy Head. Eastbourne, who were only allowed to operate within the borough boundary, claimed they should be allowed to operate the route as they were responsible for maintaining the winding road that led up from the promenade to the cliff tops. The Traffic Commissioners decided that the route should be run jointly. At the time, double-deckers were not allowed to the top due to the nature of the road, so Southdown bought two three-axled, long single-deckers that could carry more passengers. Eastbourne Corporation tried to be clever and, although the service to the top from the pier was timed at every thirty minutes alternating between the two companies, they instructed their crews to run ten minutes late on the return journey so they attracted more fares. The Traffic Commissioners took a dim view of this, revoking their licence to operate the route and handing the entire service over to Southdown.

Southdown had inherited a wide variety of vehicles on amalgamation and from the smaller companies that they subsequently took over. When these needed replacing, the company originally favoured buses produced by Tilling-Stevens and Dennis but, by the late 1920s, Leylands were chosen to supply the majority of chassis and engines. In those days Leyland was a much respected company offering a good reliable product. Single-deckers were mainly Tigers or Cubs while the doubles were Titans. They often, but not exclusively, used a local body-builder, Harrington's of Hove, to body their coaches and the Southdown name was applied in script to the sides of the coaches. Buses had the company name applied in block letters. Shorts and Beadle were two of the companies responsible for supplying early bus bodies.

The Second World War saw a break with using Leyland, as all their output was put towards the war effort. The War Department requisitioned some of the fleet to be converted into ambulances for wounded soldiers. This, along with a lack of new vehicles, led to a dire shortage of buses throughout the country. To increase loadings the seats were taken out and replaced with benches running along the sides of the buses. This left a space in the centre where up to thirty passengers could stand. As the war dragged on, the government let Guy build some austerity vehicles and Southdown purchased some of their new Arabs. When Leyland went back into production after the end of hostilities, orders were shared between the two companies for a while before Leyland regained 100 per cent of the orders. Early engines had all been petrol driven but gradually oil engines took over and some buses had their original engines changed from petrol to oil. After the war ended some bus bodies had reached the end of their useful lives, so new bodies were fitted to old chassis, extending the life of the vehicles. Perhaps the most famous were the Beadle rebuilds, where modern-looking, full-frontal bodies were fitted in place of the traditional half-cab design.

In 1946 a deal was struck with Portsmouth Corporation to share mileage run and receipts taken on a 57/43 basis, with Portsmouth having the larger share. This deal lasted until deregulation. A similar deal was struck in Brighton with Brighton, Hove & District Corporation, as well as in Crawley with the London Transport Executive.

Southdown's services were not confined to the coast and, further inland, Beacon Motor Services of Crowborough was acquired in 1954. The company divided its operating area into five regions based at Eastbourne, Brighton, Worthing, Chichester/Bognor and Portsmouth. Within these there were forty-one depots and garages in Sussex and twelve in Hampshire. These ranged from depots housing many vehicles and maintenance facilities to smaller premises known as dormitories where maybe only one bus would be parked overnight. The central works, which was originally at Freshfield Road, Brighton, became inadequate as the company grew and new central workshops were opened at Victoria Road, Portslade. There were also offices in most larger towns where holidays could be booked, parcels dropped off or collected, or a simple enquiry made.

The 1950s saw a growth in holiday trade as people shrugged off wartime austerity. At home people flocked to the seaside and Southdown converted some of their aging Guy Arabs to open-toppers to serve on routes to the top of Beachy Head and Devils Dyke. Most seafronts including Eastbourne and Brighton witnessed a row of coaches lining up on promenades during the morning, advertising afternoon trips to places of interest or evening mystery tours. Blackboards with destinations carefully written in chalk would be leant up against the wheels – never the paintwork! Trips would include other seaside towns like Hastings or long-gone attractions like Wannock Tea Gardens, just outside Eastbourne. Although they were in competition with other local coach operators, it is said that Southdown drivers did not have to try too hard to sell their tickets as Southdown's reputation for reliability and good service made their trips more attractive than their rivals.

At the end of the 1950s, Southdown owned 981 vehicles, of which 427 were coaches and 554 were buses. Leyland was the greatest supplier of these with 787 vehicles, with Guy having supplied 103. Fifty vehicles were Beadles and twenty-five Beadle-Commer. Commer accounted for fifteen vehicles and there was a single Dennis Falcon single-deck bus. The 1950s had seen the total demise of the iconic Bedford OBs. During the 1950s and 1960s Southdown benefitted from the demise of the railway, with many former rail passengers having to travel by bus. The company extended some of its routes to serve villages that no longer had a station. One of these was the service 38 that was extended from Meonstoke to Alton station. A new service 60A was also introduced to cover for the Petersfield to South Harting via Norwood rail service. The service 22 also joined up with the service 61 to provide a through service from Petersfield to Pulborough.

In 1964, the company moved its headquarters to Freshfield Road, Brighton, and in 1969 was purchased by the National Bus Company. The familiar green and cream livery was gradually lost under the darker corporate apple green of the NBC. The 1970s saw major changes within the industry, not least being the introduction of one-man operation. While many companies had opted for Leyland Atlanteans, Southdown was using Daimler Fleetlines and Bristol VRTs. In 1989 it changed hands again, becoming part of the Stagecoach Group; the livery was changed again to the white, red, orange and blue livery that covers most of the buses in the south today.

The Singles

1008 (UF 5808) was a Leyland TS2 originally fitted with a Harrington C26C body. This body was sold to Dawson, a dealer in Brixton, in 1935 and subsequently fitted to a Western SMT Regal. It is pictured here with a new Harrington C32R body with a canvas folding roof fitted in 1936. It was withdrawn in 1953 and sold to J. Light, a dealer and breaker of Lewes.

1075 (UF 9775) was a Leyland Tiger TS4 delivered in 1933. It was fitted with a Harrington C32R body. It was requisitioned by the War Department in 1940, who returned it six years later. It was withdrawn in 1955, being sold via a dealer to Salford City Welfare Department, and had ended its days by the end of 1959.

This Leyland Tiger TS2, 1061 (JK 1266), had a Park Royal C32R body. It was not bought new but entered the fleet when Southdown took over Southern Glideway of Eastbourne. The legal lettering on the side states that Southdown's registered office was at 5 Steine Street and that the vehicle had a top speed of 30 mph.

A frontal view of TS2 1061 outside Portslade works.

1085 (UF 9785) was a Leyland Tiger TS4, delivered in 1933 with a Harrington body equipped with sliding roof. It was requisitioned by the War Department in 1940 and not returned until June 1948. It was rebuilt in 1950, receiving a new 8.6-litre diesel engine. It was withdrawn in March 1957, being sold via a dealer to the Yorkshire firm of Sheppard where it lasted until the early 1960s.

Another view of a Leyland Tiger TS4, this time 1084 (UF 9784). Southdown used script for their name on the sides of coaches but buses had the company name in block capitals. It had a similar life to 1085, seen in the previous photo, being requisitioned by the War Department and not returned until June 1948. It was also withdrawn in 1957.

Not looking its best at Light's breakers yard at Lewes was 1935 Leyland Tiger TS7 1120 (CCD 720). (Courtesy A. M. Lambert)

Victoria coach station witnessed the arrival of 1935 Leyland Tiger TS7 1106 (BUF 406), fitted with a Park Royal C32R body. It played its part in the Second World War as it was converted into an ambulance in 1939. It was converted back in 1946 and had its 7.6-litre petrol engine replaced by an 8.6-litre diesel engine, fitted in 1950. It was sold in 1956 via a dealer to contractor G.E.B. Construction, where it lasted until 1958.

1142 (CCD 742) was a 1936 Leyland Tiger TS7 with a Beadle C32R body. Seen here confusingly with Express Service London–Brighton side boards and Hastings on the front destination blind. It was fitted with an 8.6-litre litre diesel engine in 1946 and rebuilt by Portsmouth Aviation in 1948. It was sold to F. Coupe & Sons of Middlewich via F. Cowley, a dealer, in 1957 and was scrapped three years later. (Courtesy A M. Lambert)

Burlingham's bodied 1159, a 1936 Leyland Tiger TS7. It was delivered with a diesel engine, converted to a 7.6-litre petrol engine in 1940, and then had another diesel engine fitted in 1950. It came with a Walman half-length sliding roof and was used on express services. It was taken out of service in 1956 and sold to a dealer.

1172 (DUF 172) was new in 1937. This Harrington-bodied vehicle was requisitioned for wartime use and was used by The Royal Army Service Corps from 1940. When it returned to Southdown after the end of hostilities, it was fitted with a Beadle C32R body. It was sold to a dealer in 1958 and is known to have finished its days in Ireland, possibly transporting miners at Tipperary.

The Singles

Perhaps unsurprisingly, DUF 174 had a similar life to its sister vehicle in the last photograph. It ended its days being sold to a dealer in this country.

9 (DUF 9), a 1937 Leyland Cheetah with Park Royal B26R bodywork with blinds removed and lettering painted out, fitted with trade plates from Manchester. Was this the last time it was seen in Sussex? (Courtesy A. M. Lambert)

This was a Park Royal B26R-bodied 1936 Leyland Cub, usually to be found in the Hayling Island area as they were light enough to cross the Langstone Viaduct. There were three of these: 10–12 (CUF 410–412).

1214 (FUF 314) was a 1939 Leyland Tiger TS8 with Harrington C32R bodywork. It was one of a batch of fourteen. Photographed at Crawley bus station. It was sold to dealer F. Cowley of Salford in March 1957.

31 (CCD 701) was a 1936 Leyland Cub with Harrington C20F bodywork.

Southdown continued to buy more Leyland Cubs and in 1938 took delivery of four more: 55–58. This was 55 (EUF 555). (Courtesy A. M. Lambert)

The following year Southdown took delivery of seven more Leyland Cubs: 15–36. 35 (DUF 35) is about to do an excursion to Alfriston in the Sussex Downs.

57 (EUF 557) was a 1938 Leyland Cub with a Harrington C20F body fitted with a folding roof, which this driver has taken advantage of. It was pictured here on Madiera Drive, Brighton.

Another Southdown touting for business for a West Sussex tour on Madeira Drive, Brighton, and another 1936 Leyland Cub, is CUF 405, this time with Harrington C14F body. Note the advertising board was leaning against the tyre and not the paintwork.

Two 1936 Leyland Cubs with Harrington's bodywork line up on Brighton seafront. In front is CUF 403, while sister vehicle CUF 404 is behind. Their two drivers are in conversation on the promenade. The latter has been preserved.

The 1930s saw a bus war with Eastbourne Buses over the lucrative route to the top of Beachy Head. A deal was done where the route was shared but Southdown were only allowed to operate single-deckers. To maximise their seating, two three-axled vehicles were purchased that allowed the length to be increased from 27 feet to 30 feet. These were Leyland Tiger TS7T with Short B40C bodies. Eastbourne Corporation were caught 'cheating' by holding their buses back ten minutes at the top of Beachy Head in an attempt to carry more passengers, but their underhand tactics cost them dear as they lost their licence to run the route and Southdown inherited 100 per cent of the trade.

Standing outside the pier was 552 (originally numbered 52), one of the two six-wheelers bought especially for the Beachy Head service. Both vehicles were withdrawn in 1952.

An offside view of a Leyland TS7T. It was parked opposite the old depot on Royal Parade. The building behind the bus was once used to store deck chairs and ended its life as a butterfly house. It has now been demolished and is part of a car park.

This 1935 Leyland Tiger TS7 was fitted with a Harrington B32R body. It was fleet no. 1420. The service 30 on the side blind was at odds with the service 32 relief shown on the front blind. It was sold in 1957 and lasted another six years in private hands.

1935 also saw the delivery of twenty-four Harrington-bodied dual-purpose vehicles. They were numbered 1400 to 1423. They had semi-coach high-backed seats, a sliding roof and luggage space on the roof reached by a ladder attached to the rear. The above was 1410, sold in 1956.

Another example of the dual-purpose Leyland Tigers was 1406. They were delivered with petrol engines, but these were swapped with the diesel engines fitted to the TS8s in 1939/40. During the Second World War they were all converted to perimeter seating, which allowed sixty passengers to board. After the war they were converted back, but had the sliding roofs sealed up and luggage racks removed.

Above: Thirty-six more Leyland Tiger TS8s were delivered in the latter part of 1938. These had Harrington B32R bodies and 8.6-litre diesel engines. The first twelve had sliding roofs. Like other buses they were altered to perimeter seating during the war. This allowed sixty passengers to squeeze on board. They were converted back to a more civilised thirty-two seats after the end of hostilities. Seen here, 1463 was withdrawn in 1957 and ended its days in Scotland in 1959.

Overleaf: Alfriston was the setting for this shot of 1478, a 1939 Leyland Tiger delivered in November 1939. It had a Harrington B32R body, but had the seating altered to perimeter seating during the war years. It was withdrawn in 1957.

Relegated to a school run was 18 (CUF 518), a 1936 Leyland Cub with Park Royal body.

Posing outside the Palace Pier Hotel near Pool Valley was 1437 (FCD 37), a Harrington B32R-bodied Leyland Tiger TS8. Delivered in 1938 it gave nearly twenty years' service, being sold in 1957 to a dealer, F. Cowley. Originally delivered with a sliding roof, this was sealed shut in 1951, as were most of the sliding roofs. During the war the forward-facing seating was removed and replaced by seating along the sides that allowed room for thirty standees, giving a capacity of sixty. It reverted to normal seating in 1948.

601 (EUF 501) was a 1938 Leyland Cheetah with a Park Royal body. It was one of five delivered that year that spent their career in the Hayling Island area, where they were light enough to traverse the Langstone viaduct.

1939 saw another six Leyland Cheetahs delivered. These were 605–10 (FUF 505–10), again with Park Royal bodies. 608 is seen here. They were bought for excursion work, as the 'Southdown' in script demonstrates. Vehicles bought for service work had the Southdown in block lettering. (Courtesy A. M. Lambert)

607 (FUF 507) was a sister vehicle to the coach in the previous image. It was photographed at Havant station – the starting point of its journey to Hayling Island.

The war years did not see any great strides in the design of buses. Twenty-five Leyland Tiger PS1s were delivered in early 1947 with Eastern Coachworks C31R bodies. This example, 1230, had been fitted with a canoe carrying rack. These were movable between buses and hired by canoe clubs and available from most coastal depots. This one was photographed in Guildhall Square, Portsmouth.

1238 (GUF 738), a Leyland tiger PS1/1 introduced in 1947 with an Eastern Coach Works C31R body, was photographed inside Lewes bus station. There were twenty-five in the class, which were soon relegated to bus work with some having their coach seats replaced with bus seating.

Another example of the class, 1242 is seen on an excursion in Portsmouth. Originally they were numbered 675–699.

During May 1947, twelve more Leyland Tiger PS1/1s were delivered with Park Royal bodies. 1253 is seen leaving Freshfield Road depot. The whole class was withdrawn in 1958.

Harrington also bodied six Leyland Tiger PS1/1 in 1947/8. They were front-entrance thirty-two seaters, numbered 1264–1269, and were fitted with sliding roofs. They were all withdrawn in 1957. 1268 was photographed leaving Freshfield Road depot.

Windover Huntingdon also bodied some 1948 Leyland Tiger PS1/1. These bodies were instantly recognisable by the lack of a canopy over the engine and mouldings around the wheels. HUF 275 was one of six (HUF 270–5, 1270–5). (Courtesy A. M. Lambert)

JUF 83 was a Dennis Falcon used on Route 47 to Hayling Island as it was light enough to go over the weak bridge linking the island with the mainland.

There were ten of these 1949 Dennis Falcons with Harrington's B30R bodywork. They were powered by petrol engines. After three years of storage from 1956, eighty-four was sold to the Salford dealer, Frank Cowley.

An offside view of a Dennis Falcon outside Havant station and about to start service 47A to Sandy Point Road on Hayling Island. Like others in its class it was withdrawn in 1956 and stored. It was eventually acquired by Petty's Television and used as a mobile showroom. It was then owned by Southsea Rowing Club, who used it to transport their boats.

A front view of a Dennis Falcon in Hilsea Garage. 91 (JUF 91) was minus its blinds, and so possibly waiting to leave the garage for the last time! It was withdrawn in 1956 and stored until 1959 when it was sold. In 1960 it was owned by R. Pratt of Hailsham, who turned it into a racing car transporter. Four years later it had become a boat transporter. It was at a breakers in 1965.

JCD 371 was one of two Bedfords with twenty-one-seat Duple bodies. They were purchased primarily for the service to Hayling Island that had a very severe weight limit on the bridge leading to it. They replaced two Falcons that could only traverse the bridge if they were empty – the passengers had to alight and walk over the bridge. It was seen here inside Portslade Works.

The post-war years saw a dramatic change in the design of coaches. This was one of the first to be delivered with an underfloor engine allowing a full front, making the half-cabs look very dated. 1809 (LCD 209) was a Duple Ambassador-bodied Leyland Royal Tiger. This one was captured in the village of Alfriston in Sussex.

The ladies seem to be enjoying themselves on this sunny day, visiting the Dicker Pottery and Alfriston. It was probably of no concern to them but they were riding on a 1952 Leyland Royal Tiger with coachwork also by Leyland. It was sold in 1963 to Roman City of Bath.

A similar vehicle to the one on the last page, but this one is having to work harder for its living, being on a South Coast Express service between Eastbourne and Bournemouth. It is pictured at Exceat in the Cuckmere Valley.

In 1952 Southdown also bought twenty Leyland Royal Tigers with Harrington C26C coachwork. Originally numbered 810–29, in 1955 they were re-numbered 1810–29 and in 1961 1610–1629. 1821, pictured here, still retains its white roof and window surrounds. It was sold in 1966 and eventually ended up in Australia on the Parramatta – Ryde bus service.

Passengers on this Harrington-bodied Royal Tiger faced a long journey as the destination blinds state that it was bound for the Lake District. Unlike the coach in the previous photograph it was painted in an all-over green livery. Like others in its class, it was converted to a forty-one seater in 1961 and withdrawn in 1966.

Ten Leyland Royal Tiger PSU1/13s with East Lancs B40R bodies were delivered in 1951/2. LUF 51 was fleet No. 1501. Originally delivered as rear entrance, they were converted to one-man operation in the late 1950s, becoming B41Fs.

1514 (MCD514) was delivered in 1953. It is a Leyland Royal Tiger with East Lancs B40C body. It was pictured at Pool Valley before setting off on service 32 via Burgess Hill, Haywards Heath and Horsted Keynes to Uckfield.

Alfriston was the setting for 1528 (MCD 528). Although delivered with a centre entrance, the class was altered to front entrance to enable one-man operation.

MUF 623 was a Leyland Tiger Cub designed for one-man operation. It had a Duple (Midland) B39F body. It was seen here inside Hilsea depot.

This driver was enjoying a quiet trip through the countryside on a Seaford to Hailsham via Alfriston trip. The location is the junction of the road to Alfriston with the A27, where Drusillas Zoo now is. He was in charge of 625, a Duple-bodied Leyland Tiger Cub delivered in 1954.

1524 (MCD 524) was one of a further batch of thirty East Lancs B40C-bodied Royal Tigers delivered in 1952/3. They were all eventually converted to one-man operation with doors moved to the front.

1300 (HUF 300) was a Leyland Tiger PS1 delivered in 1948 with a Park Royal C32R body with sliding roof. It was withdrawn in 1959. Behind it was 1001 (OUF 101), a 1955 Tiger Cub with Beadle C41C bodywork.

The late 1940s also saw the introduction of twenty-three Beadle FC32R-bodied Leyland Tiger PS1/1. 1282 was spotted in Lewes after leaving the bus station. They were built as half-cabs but converted to full fronts during 1954/5.

Above: Another of the Beadle conversions was being readied for a trip to the races at Freshfield Road depot. The whole class of twenty-three had been withdrawn by the end of 1960.

Opposite: Beadle also rebodied forty Leyland Tigers that were originally delivered with Duple half-cab bodies. The conversions took place in 1954/5. This example was photographed on a sunny day in Eastbourne, touting for business for an afternoon tour of Beachy Head and the South Downs.

In 1952, twenty Leyland Tiger TS8 chassis were delivered sporting new Beadle FC35C bodies. This example, 864, was spotted at Hilsea depot.

In 1953 Southdown reconditioned ten old Leyland TS8 chassis and equipped them with new Beadle full-front bodies. They were renumbered 645–654 in 1958 from the original 845–854. This meant that all numbers in the 8xx sequence were available to be used by the large number of Queen Marys that were on their way.

Five 1953 Leyland Royal Tigers were delivered with Duple Coronation Ambassador coachwork. This vehicle, 1645, was exhibited at the 1952 Commercial Motor Show and was the only example to be fitted with flush fitting doors. It was pictured at Hyde Park Road coach station before leaving for Brighton.

MCD 49 was another example of a Duple Coronation Ambassador-bodied Leyland Royal Tiger delivered in 1949. This one was seen in the Exceat Valley, just east of Seaford in Sussex. They seated forty-one passengers with a central door. All five of the class were sold in 1966, with this particular example going to Rhymney Transport Services.

In 1953 Southdown took delivery of more Leyland Royal Tigers with Duple C41C bodywork. This example was spotted in Seaford High Street. It was sold to Wimpey's in 1966 and subsequently exported to Malta.

1656 gives a good side view of the 1953 batch of a Duple C41C Leyland Tigers at an unknown location.

1954 saw another eleven examples delivered. They were originally numbered 1670–80 but in 1955/6 were renumbered 1835–45. The first five had Harrington Wayfarer C26C bodies, while the rest had Duple C41C bodies. In 1956 these were converted to C26C. 1835, with white roof and window surrounds, was seen here at Cavendish Place depot, Eastbourne.

1617 (LUF 617) was a Duple Ambassador C41C with sliding roof, for express services. It was photographed in Upper Rock Gardens in Brighton. Driving along with open doors would be frowned upon these days.

There were 115 of these Beadle C41C Leyland Tiger Cubs delivered between 1955 and 1957, making them one of the most common Southdown vehicles. This one, 1012, was one of the first to be delivered in May 1955. It was seen here on Madeira Drive, Brighton, waiting to start an excursion to Hastings for 8s (40p).

1023 was seen struggling up the hill from East Dean on its way to Wannock Tea Gardens. These were just outside Polegate and were a popular destination for local people and visitors alike. The site is now a small housing estate. Note the driver with a white top to his cap.

I think this is one of those great shots, not just for the Beadle-bodied Tiger Cub, but for everything around it – the traffic lights and 'keep left' bollards; the shops that could still advertise cigarettes – not to mention the British-made cars.

1037 (OUF 137) leaves Freshfield Road depot with his centre doors still open. Driving with open doors today would lead to a disciplinary hearing for the driver.

A coachload of hopeful punters set off from Lewes bus station on their way to Glorious Goodwood for an afternoon of horse racing. In charge of Beadle C41C Tiger Cub 1049 was a driver in his white summer uniform.

The Art Deco building of Cavendish Place bus depot was being renovated in this shot of 1956 Tiger Cub 1069 leaving for a trip over the South Downs. The boards outside the office are advertising trips to Brands Hatch and Fontwell Park races.

Seaford town centre was the setting for this Beadle-bodied Leyland Tiger Cub, delivered around 1964. It was one of seventy-five in the class that were lighter, more fuel efficient versions of the Royal Tiger. It was withdrawn towards the end of 1966.

Another Tiger Cub, 1051 (RUF 51) waits in Steine Road, Brighton, to pick up passengers for a day at Goodwood Races in West Sussex.

1956 saw a change in favoured chassis manufacturer and twenty-five Commers were purchased with Beadle integral bodywork. The first five, including this one pictured at Alfriston, had central doors whereas subsequent deliveries had doors at the front.

4 (RUF 104) was delivered in July 1956. The side destination boards claim it is on a London to Brighton service, while the front destination blind says Seaford. The first five had central rather than front doors with a different driver's cab window.

Another example of the class is 24 (TUF 24), delivered in September 1957 on the same service as the previous photograph. It was withdrawn in 1959.

With Portsmouth Harbour station in the background, 17 (TUF 17) is nearing the end of its trip from London.

Hyde Park Road was the setting for 15, a Beadle-Commer TS3 of integral construction with C41F body. It was photographed after arriving from Portsmouth. It was sold in 1969 to Thyssen of Llanelli.

The driver appears to be accepting a tip from a grateful passenger after arriving at Brighton's Steine Road depot with 23, a Beadle Commer.

Leyland's were still the major supplier of chassis, with 115 Tiger Cubs being delivered between 1954 and 1957. They mainly had Beadle C42C bodies but three examples (1091–3) were given C37C bodies. One of those, 1093, is pictured here before embarking on a Continental tour.

Leyland Tiger Cub, 1085, with Beadle C41C body leaves Freshfield Road, Brighton depot, bound for the races either at Brighton or Goodwood.

The next batch of Tiger Cubs with Beadle bodies were 1115–29, delivered in 1957/8. Some had thirty-seven seats, others forty-one. 1116, seen here, had thirty-seven seats and a Southdown Enthusiasts Society board displayed on the front.

Another of the batch was 1122, seen here before setting off to Ireland. The passengers on this had a bit more legroom as it was a C37F. The posters on the wall behind were advertising trips to Paris and Brussels.

A busy day at Pool Valley, Brighton, with five Leyland Titans and a Leyland Tiger TS8.

Introduced in 1961, 1700 (2700 CD) was the first of a batch of thirty Leyland Leopards (1700–29) with Harrington Cavalier C28F bodies. They were delivered with cream roofs, but these were painted green from 1962. In 1967 they were converted to C41F. 1700 was sold in 1975.

Still with its white roof was 1717 (2717 CD), another of the 1961 Harrington Cavalier-bodied Leyland Leopards. It stayed with Southdown until 1975.

1738 (8738 CD) was one of another batch of fifteen Leyland Leopards with Cavalier bodies delivered in 1961/2. It was loaned to Alder Valley, then Western National/Royal Blue, becoming their 2203 and bearing their livery. It was sold in 1974.

By 1966, Southdown had switched to Plaxton to body their Leyland Leopard coaches. Harrington, who had been used to body their vehicles, went out of business in 1966. This one was sporting a Panorama 1 body.

1968 had seen some minor design differences to Plaxton Body design, with much of the brightwork disappearing. Southdown had also changed their paintwork, doing away with the dark green skirt around the base. This was fleet No. 1243.

The Doubles

Above: Another of the rebodied TD3s was pictured here at Hyde Park Road.

Opposite: AUF 664 was in its second body when pictured here. It was a Leyland TD3 delivered in 1934 with a Short's body, which was replaced in 1947 by this East Lancs H26/26R version.

Some Short Bros-bodied 1934 TD3s were also rebodied by Beadle. 971 was photographed at Hyde Park Road depot.

East Lancs also rebodied some Leyland TD3s, including 972 seen here. By the end of the 1950s only four from the original batch remained: 960/1, which had Saunders H28/26R bodies and were based at Chichester, and 963/8, based at Portsmouth with East Lancs H26/26Rs.

Still sporting its original Short Bros body was 1935 Leyland TD4 109 (BUF 209), seen in Pevensey Road, Eastbourne. Most of the class received new bodies between 1947 and 1950. (Courtesy A. M. Lambert)

This 1935 Titan TD4, 108, originally had a Short Bros body but had this East Lancs H28/26R body fitted in 1949.

119 (BUF 219) was another of the East Lancs-rebodied 1935 Leyland TD4s. It was photographed at Hilsea Garage.

Still with its original Short Bros body was 147 (CCD 947). In 1950 it was given a Northern Counties H28/26R body. It was photographed here in Worthing.

Lewes bus station was the location of 130, an East Lancs H26/26R rebodied 1935 Leyland Titan TD4. The service 24 ran between Brighton Pool Valley and Lewes via Pyecombe, Hurstpierpoint, Hassocks and Offham.

Above: The village of Alfriston nestling in the South Downs was not built for buses, so when two meet it can get very interesting! Here 136 (BUF 236), an East Lancs-rebodied Leyland TD3 squeezes past 169, a Park Royal H28/26R rebodied Leyland Titan TD5 built in 1938 with a Short Bros body and rebodied in 1949.

Opposite: Leaving Lewes bus station bound for Seaford via Newhaven was 148 (CCD 948), a Northern Counties H28/26R version of a 1936 Leyland Titan, originally delivered with a Short Bros body. It had started its journey at Haywards Heath and travelled via Wivelsfield and Plumpton.

Beadle was responsible for bodying 142, a 1935 TD4. It was standing next to a 1953 Leyland PD2/12 with Leyland H30/26RD body at Pool Valley.

This Leyland TD5 still had its original Beadle L26/26R body when photographed at Pool Valley. In 1950 this was replaced by a Northern Counties H28/26R version.

This 1938 Leyland Titan TD5, sporting a 1950 Park Royal H28/26R body, was snapped passing a trolleybus going in the opposite direction as it made its way through the streets of Portsmouth. It was being overtaken by a Ford Prefect.

Above: 162 was a 1938 Leyland Titan TD5, given this East Lancs H28/26R body in 1950. Photographed at Lewes bus station on service 123 from Haywards Heath to Seaford.

Opposite: 160 (EUF 160), a 1938 Leyland Titan TD5, was photographed at Berwick still sporting its original lowbridge Park Royal body.

Above: 246 (GCD 46) was another of the batch of 1939 Leyland Titan TD5s delivered in 1939 with a Park Royal body. It was given an East Lancs H28/26R body in 1950 and it was sporting this when photographed on the streets of Portsmouth.

Opposite: EUF 194 was one of the original batch of TD5s delivered between 1937 and 1939 with a Beadle body, although in 1949 it was given a Park Royal H28/26R version.

Above: 225 (GCD 355) was a 1939 Leyland Titan TD5 delivered with this Park Royal highbridge body. It was to keep it for about ten years before being rebodied to extend its life.

Opposite: GCD 355 is seen again, this time at the top of School Hill in Lewes. It was now fitted with a Northern Counties H28/26R body.

259 (GCD 59), making its way through Portsmouth, was a 1939 Leyland TD5 rebodied by Northern Counties in 1950.

East Lancs also rebodied some of the TD5s originally fitted with Beadle bodies. This H28/26R version was on a local Brighton service. The trolleybus wires appear to have been removed from the poles in this photograph, which dates it to post-1961.

I had to include this shot purely for its location – unrecognisable today. It's Lewes High Street, when the railway bridge carrying the line to Uckfield crossed it. At the time it was also the A27, the main road between Eastbourne and Brighton. The hump-back bridge did terrible things to car passengers' stomachs! Oh yes, and it's a Park Royal-bodied Titan!

Was this the end for fleet No. 214, Beadle-bodied TD5? With blinds removed and wearing trade plates, was it about to embark on its final journey?

400 (GCD 974). It was one of 100 Guy Arabs delivered between 1943 and 1946 with a Northern Counties body. It was one of seven that originally had low-bridge bodies, but in 1951 it was given a East Lancs H28/26R body that came from Leyland Titan TD2 958 (UF 9758). It was withdrawn in June 1963. Leyland had been forced to stop producing bus chassis during the Second World War, with all their output going towards the war effort. With dire shortages of buses affecting services towards the end of hostilities, Guy were allowed to build buses to meet the demand.

Brighton's Pool Valley was the scene for 422, a Guy Arab II delivered in 1944. Originally it had H30/26R bodywork, but was converted to H26/28R in August 1949. It was re-engined and sold in September 1957.

A good side view of a 1944 Guy Arab II, 439, in Hyde Park Road depot. In 1959 it was converted to open-top and operated on the 102 route between Ferring and Shoreham until March 1964 when it was sold.

440 (GUF 140) was a Northern Counties H28/26R Guy Arab II delivered in October 1944. It was converted to open-top in 1957. (Courtesy A. M. Lambert)

456 (GUF 156) was a 1945 Guy Arab II with Northern Counties H28/26R bodywork. (Courtesy A. M. Lambert)

Working a relief to Alfriston was 457 (GUF 157), a Guy Arab.

Standing outside the bus station in Pevensey Road, Eastbourne, was this 1945 Guy Arab II with Northern Counties bodywork. Bobby's of Eastbourne, which is advertised on the side, stood where Debenham's trades today on Terminus Road.

474 (GUF 174) was a 1945 Weymann-bodied Guy Arab II. It was withdrawn in 1958. It is pictured next to a 1934 Leyland TD3 delivered with a Short H26/24R body, but in 1949 was given this Beadle H28/26R body.

Hyde Park Road was the location for this photograph of a 1945 Guy Arab with Weymann. It was one of a batch of twenty-two similar vehicles.

491 (GUF 191) was another Guy Arab II, bodied by Weymann and delivered in January 1945. Seen here at Hyde Park Road depot.

An unusual angle showing roof details of 487 (GUF 387), a 1945 Weymann-bodied Guy Arab II at Chichester bus station. The photograph was taken in the days when advertising of alcohol was not frowned upon and definitely not illegal.

This 1945 Guy Arab II, 490, was sporting a Weymann H30/26R body. It was parked in Hilsea Garage next to a 1955 Morris 10 cwt van.

The post-war years saw the renewed production of Leyland buses with PD1s. Bodywork had not evolved much during the war years as this 1946 Park Royal H28/26R testifies. It was seen at Hailsham on service 15 (now a 98), jointly run with Maidstone & District.

Another Park Royal-bodied 1946 Leyland PD1 is seen outside the bus station in Pevensey Road, Eastbourne.

A look inside the bus station at Pevensey Road, Eastbourne. A group of ladies in their summer dresses wait to board their bus for a day out, although probably not on 275 (GUF 75), the Titan PD1 being bound for East Grinstead via Uckfield.

With Watney's Brown Ale being advertised, 280, a 1946 Leyland Titan PD1, leaves for the village of Jevington nestled in the South Downs.

1947 saw delivery of twenty-four more Leyland Titan PD2/1As, but with Leyland H28/26R bodies. Had the conductor of this service just changed the destination blind ready for the return journey as it had just arrived at Eastbourne station from Hastings via Herstmonceux and Hailsham, considering was the last stop before entering Pevensey Road bus station?

HCD 915 was the last in the batch of twenty-five Leyland PD1As delivered in 1947 with Leyland's own H28/26R bodies.

New in 1948 was 319 (JCD 19), another Leyland Titan PD2/1 with Leyland H28/26R body. It was one of a class of eighty. Hilsea Garage was the venue for this photograph.

320 (JCD 20) was another 1948 PD2/1 with an altered destination screen that had a separate screen for the route number. It was pictured under the trolleybus wires in Portsmouth after making its way from Petersfield station.

I make no apologies for the inclusion of another shot of 320, this time passing the Palace Cinema in Commercial Street, Portsmouth, as there is plenty of other interest in the shot. *Tanganyika* starring Johnny Dark dates this image to 1954.

Another of the eighty Titan PD1s – this one in Pevensey Road, Eastbourne. The board on the outside wall advertises the service 12 to Brighton, while the bigger board inside extols their tours to Blackpool.

Opposite: On a local route to Woodingdean was 341 (JCD 41), another of the 1948 Leyland PD1s with Leyland's own H28/26R bodies passing through a very leafy Brighton.

Plenty of passengers are waiting for a bus in the opposite direction as 346 (JCD 46) passes by on its way to Petersfield station.

349 (JCD 49) Leyland PD2/1 sits at Pool Valley while 714 (KUF 714), a 1951 PD2/12, waits to do a relief to Portsmouth and Southsea.

Staying in Portsmouth, 344 (JCD 44) passes the Palace Picture House on Commercial Street (renamed Guildhall Walk) on Route 31 from Brighton to Southsea.

A very bright summer day sees Leyland Titan PD2/1 at Portsmouth. Beacon Coach Tours, formerly of Crowborough and advertised on the side of the bus, was bought by Southdown in 1954, although they had been controlling them since 1949.

358 is in Portslade Works and is in need of a bit of TLC to the top nearside corner.

Looking very smart and devoid of adverts, which probably means that 379 (JCD 79) was photographed soon after delivery in 1948 or after a repaint.

About to descend School Hill in Lewes was 382 (JCD 82), another PD2/1 on service 123 from Haywards Heath to Seaford.

In a scene from another age with a thatched petrol station, with pumps where you are served by an attendant, was 389 (JCD 89), making its way through the South Downs to Alfriston.

384 (JCD 84) was another of the batch of eighty Leyland-bodied PD2/1s delivered in 1948; it was parked in Pevensey Road, Eastbourne when this photo was taken.

After the end of the Second World War, Southdown did not revert to buying Leylands entirely. Northern Counties bodied twelve Guy Arab IIIs delivered in 1948/9. These were numbered 500 to 511. 502 differed from the rest of the class as it had standee windows above the usual ones. It was pictured in Brighton on a hot day and drivers of both vehicles had their windscreen open.

503 was another Northern Counties Guy Arab III here on a local Brighton service. Behind it was a Brighton Corporation 1938 AEC with Weymann body.

506 (JCD 506) was a Guy Arab III delivered in 1949 with a Northern Counties H28/26R body. It was parked beside a Leyland Titan PD2/1 in Hilsea depot.

Another of the batch of twelve Northern Counties Guy Arab IIIs, 507 was overtaking a Portsmouth Corporation Leyland.

A wide shot of Pool Valley bus station sees Guy Arab III with Northern Counties H28/26R body 508 (JCD 508) leaving for Coldean while open-top GUF 120, a 1944 Guy Arab II, waits to start a trip to Henfield via Devils Dyke.

The entrance to Pool Valley is via a very narrow road, as demonstrated by this 1955 Guy Arab IV with Park Royal H31/26RD bodywork.

514 (OUF 514) was a 1955 Guy Arab IV with Park Royal H31/26RD bodywork, seen heading along the A27 near Berwick.

Another Guy Arab IV was 518 (OUF 518), with Park Royal H31/26RD bodywork. This one was parked at Edward Street depot, Brighton.

A busy scene at Eastbourne's Pevensey Road bus station (now a nightclub) saw 524, a Guy Arab IV with Park Royal H33/26RD body, leaving on service 25 to Brighton via Lewes. It was one of a batch of twenty-five delivered in 1956.

Arriving at Lewes bus station was 524 (PUF 624), a 1956 Guy Arab IV with Park Royal H33/26RD bodywork en route from Brighton to Sheffield Park station.

School Hill, Lewes, saw Guy Arab IV 526 (PUF 626) on service 28, which was a local service linking housing estates around the town.

Another Guy Arab IV, 532 (PUF 632), was photographed at Lewes bus station before setting off for Eastbourne via Hailsham.

This is a scene that has changed very little since this photograph was taken about sixty years ago. It is Exceat Valley where the River Cuckmere flows into the sea. 537 (PUF 636) was one of a batch of thirty-five Guy Arab IVs delivered in 1956 with Park Royal H33/26RD bodies.

Parked on the pavement outside the depot on Royal Parade, Eastbourne, 539 poses for this side view of a Park Royal-bodied Guy Arab IV.

Employed on a local service in Lewes was 547 (PUF 647), a Guy Arab IV with Park Royal H33/26RD body. This bus was fitted with a sliding door instead of the normal 'jack-knife' type.

These Guy Arab IVs were allotted to Brighton, Eastbourne and Worthing depots, which accounts for all the images being in the east of the operating area. Lewes is the location of another example, 548, of a Guy Arab IV with Park Royal H33/26RD bodywork.

KUF 700 was a unique vehicle. It was a 1950 Leyland Titan PD2/12 with Northern Counties body, purchased initially for the Eastbourne–London express service. Unfortunately it was prone to roll at higher speeds, inducing sickness in many of the passengers. It was first seen at the 1950 Commercial Motor Show. In January 1952 it was converted to FH32/26RD and then FCH28/22RD five months later. It was demoted to operating a school service in Portsmouth.

Another view of KUF 700, parked at Hyde Park road depot.

In 1951/2, forty-four Leyland Titan PD2/12s were delivered with Leyland's own H32/26RD bodies. These were the first to be delivered with the 30-foot-long and 8-inch-wide chassis allowed by new relaxed laws. 702 was pictured at Hilsea depot between two 1948 PD2/1s.

Above: Traffic was heavy in Brighton as the driver of 705, a 1951 Leyland Titan PD2/12, set out on a long trip to Portsmouth.

Opposite: 707, another Leyland PD2/12, turns right before ascending the high street in Lewes on its way to Brighton.

Hilsea depot was the location of 709, a Titan PD2/12. The advertising of cigarettes and tobacco was a good source of income for many bus companies in the 1950s and 1960s.

A rear view of 1951 Leyland Titan PD2/12, with Leyland's own H32/26RD bodywork; 711 (KUF 711) inside Hyde Park Road depot.

Under a mass of trolleybus wires outside Southsea station was 721 (KUF 721) on service 31 from Brighton.

Above: Berwick X roads on the A27 saw 726, a Titan PD2/12, pass 1526, a 1953 Leyland Royal Tiger, on service 126.

Opposite: 733 (LUF 233) was one of the same class as the previous image. It was seen at Exceat Valley between Brighton and Eastbourne. This was a very hilly route, not only having to cross the Seven Sisters Cliffs but also steep hills in and out of East Dean and the long, steep drop down into Eastbourne.

719 (KUF 719), a 1951 PD2/12 with Leyland H32/26RD body, was seen under the trolleybus wires in Portsmouth after a journey from Brighton via Worthing, Littlehampton and Chichester.

In 1953, Southdown bought ten Leyland-bodied Leyland PD2/12s. These were numbered 745 to 754. The last in the series was seen in Portsmouth on service 40, bound for Petersfield. Behind it is BCD 358, a Southdown Northern Counties-rebodied TD5.

Also in 1953, ten Leyland Titan PD2/12s were purchased with Northern Counties H30/26RD bodies. These were numbered 755–764. 755 was passing a window cleaner's hand cart when it was snapped on this Portsmouth street.

Another of the class, 762, was crossing Shoreham Bridge, bound for Brighton from Petersfield when snapped here.

In 1956, Southdown bought twelve Beadle-bodied Leyland Titan PD2/12s. These were H33/26RD. 778 was photographed at Lewes bus station.

Another shared route with M&D was the 122 Gravesend–Brighton, which was the longest bus route in the country at the time. This necessitated crews driving the other operator's vehicles over part of the route. 782 was nearing the end of its long journey at Lewes when photographed here.

During 1956/7, another twenty-four Leyland PD2/12s were purchased. These had East Lancs H33/26RD bodies. They were numbered 789 to 812. Here 802 is seen at Seaford making its way to Eastbourne from Brighton.

Still at Seaford, going in the opposite direction, was another of the class, 807. It had stopped outside the local office that boasted of operating a parcels service. A mystery drive could also be booked there.

This was a Leyland PD3, 823 (TCD 823) with Northern Counties bodywork. These were the last front-engine vehicles to be bought by Southdown.

411, photographed at Pool Valley on service 12C to Newhaven, had been delivered in 1964. It has styling differences compared to the example in the previous photograph. The NBC logos on the sides of both vehicles in the photograph puts the date of this image to be post-1969.

Another view, taken in NBC days at Pool Valley, saw 1965 Titan PD3 BUF 280C alongside a Northern Counties Daimler Fleetline.

Open-Toppers

820 was a 1929 Leyland Titan TD1 with a Brush body. (Courtesy A. Lambert)

Portslade Works was the site for this shot of 1929 Leyland Titan TD1 with Brush body. This was not a conversion, as was the case for the buses in the images to follow; it is how it was ordered and delivered. This bus is now preserved.

447 (GUF 147) was converted to open-top in March 1945. It was a Guy Arab II built in 1945 with a Park Royal H30/26R body. It became O30/26R in the 1950s, being withdrawn in 1959.

467 (GUF 167) was another Park Royal O30/26R conversion of the original H30/26R body on a 1945 Guy Arab II chassis. It lasted until 1964 when it was withdrawn.

Parked by the Queens Hotel in Eastbourne was 468 (GUF 168), another of the fleet of Guy Arab II open-toppers.

497 (GUF 397) was a Guy Arab II new in 1946 with a Park Royal H30/26R body. It was only six years old when converted to open-top O30/26R. It was withdrawn in July 1964.

Open-topper Guy Arab II 410 started life in 1944 with a Park Royal H30/26R body. It was converted to open-top in January 1951 and withdrawn in April 1959.

Busy times for the open-top services to the top of Beachy Head as this crowded relief service shows. The Guy Arab II, 412, was being followed by a Bedford OB as it passes the 7th Duke of Devonshire's statue at the top of Devonshire Place, Eastbourne. Note the lack of any road markings.

Brighton's Pool Valley was the starting point for a trip to Devil's Dyke. 421, a 1944 Guy Arab, was originally fitted with a Northern Counties H30/26R body before being converted to open-top O28/26R in 1957. It was sold in 1964.

A very busy scene at Eastbourne pier sees the conductor of 424 (GUF 124) finding time to lean against the pole on the platform and watch the world go by.

The end of the route for buses going to the top of Beachy Head is this turn round just past the Beachy Head Hotel. 423 has successfully completed the steep climb up from the promenade and is having a rest before starting its low-geared descent. The 1944 Guy Arab II had been converted to open-top in 1959 and served for five years before being sold in 1964 to a dealer in Salford.